Shopping Cart Chronicles

with

Tales of a Drunken Shopping Cart

(and other shopping cart adventures)

ADRIENNE VERONESE

Veronese Press

an imprint

Cover design by Bradley Wind

with photo contributions
by James D. Schlachter, Jr.

Another drunken shopping cart sleeps off
a wasted Friday night.

Some things in small town America just
don't change.

Remember kids, never leave a friend alone next to an open body of water when he's been drinking.

This is how tragedies happen.

He'd always dreamed of hooking up with one of the skinny ones, but it only led to waking up finding he'd passed out in the bushes. Yet again.

He thought he was good to roll but his drinking buddies knew better. They watched him leave the bar and faceplant himself in the bushes. Rather than help him out, they snapped pictures and posted them on Instagram.

He woke ass-over-teakettle in the Kmart
parking lot unable to remember a thing
about the night before. It was weeks before
he learned he'd gone out drinking on a
Saturday night and once again ended up
pole dancing like a damn fool.

They're going to hate themselves in the morning.

Having realized he was born into a life of
rampant consumerism, he succombed to
his baser instincts & began frequenting
the local strip trees act.

He soon found himself killing time in the
company of various assorted misfits watching
bare trees shake their limbs for anyone willing
to pay the price.

PART ONE

Feeling bluer than blue, he packed his things
& left, spending the first night in an out-of-
the-way place. But where would he go from
there?

PART TWO

His folks always said he'd end up dead in a ditch somewhere.

Daylight fades and the fog drifts in as she
contemplates the choices she's made in life that
have brought her to this point: Standing beneath
a street lamp on the cheating side of town.

Late season blackberries have fermented on
the vine & drunken shopping carts are taking
advantage of the cheap high.

There's no end in sight to the Drunken Shopping Cart riots as residents struggle to clean up the mess and rumors swirl about a possible curfew for all drunken shopping carts.

No cart is an island entire of itself. He wished
he'd remembered that before getting stuck on
one after finishing a round at the brewery.
He had to piss and there were no bushes on
that island.

The Runaway

(with apologies to Robert Frost)

Remember kids, stay off the grass. Grass is a gateway drug that leads to napping.

He wanted to hang with the Big Dogs; to show the world he could pull a heavy load just like them. But it wasn't until he found himself sandwiched between two of them that he realized why they'd singled him out and pretended to include him.

What if you threw a barbecue party
and nobody showed up; not even
the lawn furniture?

They called him "Poof." As if being lavender
was a bad thing. He was born lavender. But life
in a small town isn't easy if you're different. He
often found himself alone, gazing northward
where he'd heard people were more accepting.
Somewhere someday he'd find a place where
he fit in. A place where he belonged.

A place he could call home.

"Go green," they said. "You can move someplace cool like Eureka. Everybody's green there." But something must have gotten lost in translation, because everybody wasn't green there. They were ON the green. There's a difference.

A big difference.

Women complain about being cat-called by men when they're out in public. But they have no idea what it's like to be treated like a garbage can when you're just standing around passing the time with a park bench.

He'd forgotten how many times he'd been
eighty-sixed from the farmer's market.
But he was hoping by arriving in the bike lane
no one would recognize him. Maybe they'd
think he was one of those new recumbent bikes.
Or French. No one recognizes the French.

How long had he been telling people he could
have made something of his life? Could have
worn a hard hat and done an honest day's work.
And how long had it been since people had
stopped listening to his excuses for not just
doing it? The work was there; he just couldn't
stay off the junk food long enough to feel
up to the task.

"Don't shoot," he said as she took aim. "Black carts matter." She didn't even lower the camera. Not until she got what she wanted. And then walked away without a word of explanation. He turned his gaze back to the field and thought once more about white priviledge.

The only thing more useless than a coat hook at the top of a restroom door for the handicapped is a bus schedule up too high for anyone rolling on wheels to read it.

Sure, he didn't mind admitting he sometimes hid behind the bushes. He knew better than anyone how far he'd fallen. And though he wasn't proud, he did have his dignity and just didn't want anyone to see him like this.

He had that cautious optimism one often feels
when about to embark on an uphill climb
down an unpaved road.

He had dreamed of nothing but freedom, of what must lie beyond the shopping center he had known all his life. But once again his efforts to go outside the perimeter were thwarted when his wheels locked up, leaving him with that same familiar longing.

It had been his dream to one day make it to sunny Southern California, where palm trees swayed in the warm breezes and it was impossible to freeze. And for once he didn't have to worry about the penguins.

She stood staring at Goodwill's window display
and thought of how it always embarrassed her
when her mom took her thrift store shopping for
back-to-school clothes. She'd give anything
to be able to afford thrift store prices now.
And to have Mom back.

It was the last thing he expected. He'd hit the limits of his powers. Who knew it would be something as simple as a curb that would bring his plans to a dead stop?

He thought he would blend in when he got
to the city, become invisible in the sea of
others just like him. But by nightfall
he realized his vulnerability only made him
stand out. There really is nowhere to hide
from that.

The problem with hiring non-union labor to operate heavy machinery is that workers are always screwing around, and there's invariably one slacker who gets drunk on the job and has to be carried across the street to the bus stop.

"Lean on me." The song played on a continual loop in his head as he rolled. It was not the kind of ear worm he needed when he was feeling so alone on his journey. Having just admitted to himself he wasn't nearly as strong as he liked to pretend, he saw the bush waiting for him and realized he'd never really been alone.

Once again, he managed to fall for the old
"Let's play hide-and-seek" ploy.
While his back was turned, they ditched him
by jumping on the bus, leaving him
to find his way back on his own.

Sure, she'd thought about moving to the trailer
park, but what would her kids think? She'd
gotten used to their dad calling her
a deadbeat pothead living off the dole,
but she didn't think she could take it if her kids
started thinking of their mom as trailer trash.

He knew he was supposed to stay with the others, knew how important it was that he pull his own weight. But he just needed a little down-time, a minute to himself to think about what he'd seen. Why didn't anyone ever talk about things like that? Why was he expected to just hold it in and act like it didn't really matter?

He just kept telling himself as long as he had
plenty of toilet paper and a place to use it he'd
be okay.

The note on the windshield chilled him:

"When it started it was only one or two of us at a time. By the time we figured out what was happening they were taking us by the truckload and it was too late to do anything about it. Some say they're taking us to the African continent. Others are convinced we're headed for the FEMA camps."

Finding the perfect place to sleep for the night, he'd just gotten the door open when he heard someone coming. Cops? Thuggies? Raptors? He decided to stand perfectly still in case it was raptors, having heard they can't see you unless you're moving.

In case you were wondering, no shopping carts were harmed in the making of this book.

Some of them may have been chased off to another part of the county, however. Because that's a thing we do.

www.ingramcontent.com/pod-product-compliance
Lightning Source LLC
Chambersburg PA
CBHW041226270326
41934CB00001B/19